HER BOOK

JO SHAPCOTT

Her Book

Poems 1988–1998

faber and faber
LONDON·NEW YORK

First published in 2000
by Faber and Faber Limited
3 Queen Square London WCIN 3AU
Published in the United States by Faber and Faber Inc.
a division of Farrar, Straus and Giroux Inc., New York

Photoset by Wilmaset Ltd, Wirral
Printed in England by Clays Ltd, St Ives plc

A CIP record for this book
is available from the British Library

ISBN 0-571-20183-0

2 4 6 8 10 9 7 5 3 1

To Her Book

All my books are little,
but dear to me. This one
goes to London without me
under plain cover, or on screen,

disk, by phone. Shove off
tiny one: take with you, then,
the whiff of angels' shit, the taste
of fresh print. Do better than I can,

plan how you'll find yourself
in my beloved's hands, murmur
a brief word of introduction
then breathe yourself in his ear.

Choose just the spot
on his round shelves to nestle,
blushing under the princess of dedications
right there, verso, in my own scrawl.

I'll stay here, indoors, a fine sweat
all I can muster to stave off the gods.
Some days I just do anything – sneeze
trip, shake hands – and they raise

hell, throw thunderbolts, push
me into traffic, get me mugged.
Whatever you do, small book,
I'll fall short: I'm tired

this autumn, cold, all
early chilblains, red eyed
and ashamed. Go on then, darling,
without me and be very, very good.

Contents

ELECTROPLATING THE BABY

Hubei Province Tornado

Mrs Yang has experienced
an air adventure. The tornado
that uprooted trees lifted
the umbrella-holding woman
several hundred yards high
into the sky. She crossed
the Jiuda River. She was carried
for five hundred and fifty yards
then landed slowly. Strangely,
though she was injured by hailstones,
she was intact.

With the Big Tray

With the big tray
Hilary had to mind the tea service
at each end of the long march
up the staircase (those places
by the newel posts where her hips
had to angle and re-angle
at the new levels). Then
there was an impasse
at the bedroom door
where really another person was needed
to get a grip on the ebony handle.
In the event an elbow served
and after wriggling and clinking
round the door like a belly dancer
she found herself inside,
foolish on the Moroccan rug.
There had been an audience:
a housefly was swooping by the lilac
in mother's clover vase – the one
Nicholas had thrown for her.
The sun constructed an avenue
to the bedside table
and now the housefly played
boomerang in and out of the light.
Hilary surprised herself by breaking wind.
Secretly, her large smell
made her feel as real and salty
as a merchant adventurer
but she would take something for it
from the bathroom cabinet anyway.

[4]

She set the tray down by the bed
noting as she did the ornate little table.
It had been made by a local craftsman
and she had, at first, been impressed
by what she interpreted
as the mark of difficulty
that its execution had left on his face.
Now there were more or less
three white rings on the walnut veneer.

Lies

In reality, sheep are brave, enlightened
and sassy. They are walking clouds
and like clouds have forgotten
how to jump. As lambs they knew.
Lambs jump because in their innocence
they still find grass exciting.
Some turf is better for tiptoeing
say the lambs. Springy meadows
have curves which invite fits
of bouncing and heel-kicking
to turn flocks of lambs
into demented white spuds boiling in the pot.
Then there is a French style of being a lamb
which involves show and a special touch
at angling the bucking legs. Watch carefully
next time: Lambs love to demonstrate –
you won't have to inveigle.
Eventually, of course, lambs grow trousers
and a blast of wool
which keeps them anchored to the sward.
Then grass is first and foremost
savoury, not palpable.
I prefer the grown sheep: even when damp
she is brave, enlightened and sassy,
her eye a kaleidoscope of hail and farewell,
her tail her most eloquent organ of gesture.
When she speaks, it is to tell me
that she is under a spell, polluted.
Her footwear has been stolen

and the earth rots her feet.
In reality she walks across the sky
upside-down in special pumps.

Late Snow

A cold spring:
the violet was flawed on the lawn.
   ELIZABETH BISHOP

With cold air advancing from the Arctic
a depression slid over the Irish Sea:
in Cambridge cricketers couldn't grip,
all routes over the Pennines were closed,
power lines tumbled in the Yorkshire Dales.

The sheep liked the snow; it suited their cryptic
coloration. They lived in ice caves like new beasts:
ice breath, ice fleece, rumination and travail –
but their tongues got stuck on the ice
as their own bloody waters froze around their lambs.

Now, in summer, I listen for cold drinks,
I root in cocktails, hold chilled tea to the light.
I'm looking for an ice cube streaked like a humbug
to hold inside my cheek for the slow melt,
until I feel hooves flutter on my tongue.

1953

Through the pregnancy I can't remember a whine
from my mother; she gave up smoking, put alphabet
paper on the spare room walls, forbore to strike
my brother, tried not to smoke, nor breathe in smog.
That's the sort of thing which puts an obligation
on you. She risks her life, she suffers;
it's all up for friendship or equality: your guilt
goes whizzing like a satellite.

                    But it still
wasn't wrong to be born in 1953 (though it was a myopic
year, full of the coronation illusion). My mum
held me up at the hospital window to see the great
procession, so she said. She admired the true
beauty of the Queen and her courage so soon
after the old King died.

                    My mum had a bully
of an illness after I was born, went home to no
carpet and an urgency to go back to work.
I went too in 1953, under her arm like a book.
Teachers were scarce; it was a small defect
to go along with a new baby, the prize
that was soon to become myself.

Lunula

Men may dyen of ymaginacioun
So depe may impressioun be take.
CHAUCER

Gold crescent moon, the lunula, battle charm
of naked Celtic warriors in a time
   when pebbles of soft ore were pulled out
      wet from the rivers of County Wicklow.

Through days and days of blow after blow to make
what's here before our eyes in the hammered face:
   those goldsmiths knew how beating gold will
      polish it up to a mirror-surface.

Sometimes at night I picture a fighting Celt:
around his neck the lunula shows me such
   an image of my face, as yellow,
      grimacing, strange to me as the devil's.

Birthday Surprise

As Daddy straightened the last candle
his thumb smudged the blue icing-sugar seven.
I opened my mouth wide to scream
but the surprise of a trickle down my leg
killed the noise. 'Power!' I was thinking,
'A puddle on the rug.' Then Mother
pulled out a tissue and blotted the wet shape
so carefully mapped and steaming on the Wilton –
my Florida, my Amazon, my Indies.

Venus Observes Herself

Her smile
makes her feel prickly –
it's lopsided like a guitar:
she wants rid of that half-curve
which seems puffy to her touch.

Her way would be clear to seventh
Heaven if she could master
this art of arriving on shells
with poise
and a waist.

She's working towards
an increase in breast/nipple ratio,
an imperceptible up-tilt
which would balance the economy
of her happinesses, cut
into her griefs like a science
secure her potential like a frame.

Now she rises:
the shell razes the water –
the Seasons advance clenching garments.

The Mug

The mug is cast in earthenware
and coloured like pale stone, the usual shade
for mixing eggs, drinking or watering plants.

Around it, in dark brown, some people stroll –
Egyptians? – all in profile looking right
(though there is one who's facing widdershins
but slightly turned, as though about to follow
the others' lead). Some bend to long curved jars;
one raises something, one holds out papyrus
with a smooth arm. These gyral figures share
the same suggestion of a slight breast's curve;
the same androgynous hips; the same blunt hair;
the knotted cloth around the waist, the same.

The handle has a bite snapped from its arc
where you can see the clay in cross-section.
It's not so bad – you can still pick it up
by bridging the brief gap with three tight knuckles
and hanging on, with your thumb and little finger,
firm as a flying buttress, for dear life.

Inside the mug the rings of tea show brown
against the stone – as if to demonstrate
age to an expert, like the rings through logs
or at the ivory base of a whale's tooth.

Saving String

On Piccadilly
you can't get away with it –
bending for a piece of string spotted from
six brisk paces away; picking it up
as carefully as the tipsy man
a dropped halfpenny;

stretching it right out
at arm's length to test the width.
Then over and over the cupped left hand,
winding it home. Get away with it
he did and in great style: all of us
on the pavement

felt our own desires
to pick up string begin to quicken.
He had set something rolling; he could
have led us as willing followers
in any campaign for saving string –
whatever he liked.

Throughout he would be
nothing without this passion
as we would be nothing. He trod the ground
at Piccadilly like a carpet
of camomile, that was the secret
and he swung his stick

squat and polished
resting the brass tip every
other step as if pointing out one
particular lepidoptera

lying perfectly disguised among
the camomile leaves.

Old fashioned rhetoric
of Chiltern Hills and gentlemen's
clubs which allows protected characters
to potter in safety and wind string,
a brew of order and avarice
which says I have this and this
but never enough string.

The Old Man and the Finches

Bird chaff creates dusting and now
there are more chances to forget things
at the supermarket: cuttle, sand, seeds.
The old man cleans the cage floor
with a small stick, his eye
so hard to the bars that the crêpe
under his lashes dents for minutes.

This passion for breeding pairs
is a hazard at any latitude
as he found when watching *Darwin*
on TV – see! A fellow of the same order:
not an aviarist, but a viewer
in the same outdoors where cameras click
like the latch on the cage.

His breeding's not working;
the Zebra Finches are getting fractious
in their soiled nest box: 'Dirty habits.
Can't put up with that sort of filth.'
The account lengthens against them
but the Waxbills, though barren,
are uncommon clean.

Beyond the bars, science
wants to fact him with a new theory
too complex, he says, for words.
Evolution now moves in jerks,
animals adapt in rapid response
to even more rapidly changing surroundings.
An idea to give him migraine.

But watch his old man's hand
envelop the smallest finch,
see him squinny through the magnifying glass.
He is grumbling, 'Can't get at it,'
as he clips at claws he cannot focus on.
Observe the crêpe under his eyes drop,
evolving in magic jumps to bone.

Love in the Lab

One day
the technicians
touched souls

as they exchanged
everyday noises
above the pipette.

Then they knew
that the state of molecules
was not humdrum.

The inscriptions
on the specimen jars
which lined the room in racks
took fire in their minds:

what were yesterday
mere hieroglyphs
from the periodic table

became today urgent proof
that even here –
laboratory life –
writing is mystical.

The jars glinted under their labels:
it had taken fifteen years
to collect and collate them.

Now the pair were of one mind.
Quietly, methodically
they removed the labels

from each of the thousands
of jars. It took all night.

At dawn, rows of bare glass
winked at their exhausted coupling
against the fume cupboard.

Using their white coats
as a disguise
they took their places at the bench
and waited for the morning shift.

Electroplating the Baby

Of the Egyptians the rich alone
were capable of having it done.

The cadavers were immersed
in antiputrescible baths

and then swathed by the relatives
in thousands of bandages.

In our time the art of embalming
has not made much advance:

are our processes so imperfect
as to dull our inclination?

Or do we relish the privacy of dust?
In answer one physician proposes

electro-metallurgy as *the* way
to obtain indestructible mummies.

He metallises our entire cadaver.
He encloses it in an envelope

of bronze, copper, nickel, silver or gold
according to the wealth or caprice

of those who survive.
Does this waken your curiosity?

Do you wish to know
how Dr Variot proceeds?

In a double frame with four uprights
connected top and bottom by four square plates

is the body of a child which has been
perforated with a metal rod.

One end of the rod abuts
against the arch of the cranium

the other is inserted as a pivot
in a metallic bearing at the base of the frame.

The frame support is a conductor of electricity.
The uprights and connecting wires

are carefully insulated
with gutta percha.

The electric current is furnished
by three small 'chaudron' thermo-electric batteries.

A circular toothed metallic contact
descends from the top plate and rests

lightly on the vertex of the cadaver.
The lover surface of the feet

and the palms of the hands
rest upon two contacts.

Before immersing this apparatus
in the electro-metallurgic bath,

it is necessary to render the body
a good conductor of electricity.

To this effect the operator
sprays the skin of the cadaver

with a solution of nitrate of silver
by means of a homely apparatus –

the atomiser used by ladies
for perfuming themselves.

This operation having been performed
the skin becomes of an opaque black

and the silver salt has penetrated
as far as to the derma.

Next the silver salt must be reduced:
that is to say, separated from its oxide

(to do this is very difficult).
The frame is placed under a glass bell

in which a vacuum has been formed,
and into which vapours of white phosphorus

dissolved in sulphide of carbon
are afterwards allowed to enter

(this is a dangerous operation
like all operations in which phosporus

in solution plays any part whatever).
Then the skin of the cadaver

is of a greyish white.
There is nothing left to do now

but to proceed as rapidly as possible
to the metallisation. To this effect

the frame is immersed in a bath
of sulphate of copper

(we need not describe this operation
which is known to all).

Under the influence of the electric current
the deposition of the metal goes on

uninterruptedly. The molecules
of metal deposit on the skin

and soon form thereon a continuous layer
(the operator must regulate

the passage of electricity with great care
in order to prevent a granular deposit

having but little adhesion).
By shifting the contacts properly

the operator will substitute for the skin
a coating of copper

which will take on the pattern
of all the subjacent parts.

By attentively watching
the thickness of the deposit

upon the face, hands and all
the delicate parts of the body,

a faithful mould will be obtained
that will exactly recall

the details of conformation
and the tints of the physiognomy.

A deposit of from half
to three quarters of a millimetre

offers sufficient strength
to resist external bendings and blows.

A thickness of from half
to three quarters of a millimetre

ought not to be exceeded
for the metallic covering

of the face and hands
which will be thus perfectly moulded.

Upon the trunk, the abdomen, the neck
and the first segments of the limbs

the integral preservation
of the plastic forms is much much less important.

What is the the future in store
for this process of mummification?

It would be impossible to say.
It is infinitely probable

that metallised cadavers
will never figure

except in small numbers
for a long, long time to come.

Fun with Robert and Elizabeth

Sitting down in the draught was distracting.
It was distracting in itself to have
to stay with cousins when you went away;
their house was too close to the thoroughfare.
Even now the troops passed on their march
by the window, having to adhere
to the autumn training routine designed to make
men of granite: bones, skin, muscles
and every item in the kitbag stone.
But distraction could be fun with Robert
and Elizabeth laughing at the simplest jokes
about the things to be seen through the window,
chuckling at the rich sounds from outside.
Towards lunchtime they would become more terse,
each listening to interpret the faint sounds
of the other's scourings on the paper.

Elizabeth Looks at Robert

*For a woman to hang down her head like a lily through
life, and 'die of a rose in aromatic pain' at her death, – to
sit or lounge as in a Book of Beauty, and be 'defended' by
the strong and mighty thinkers on all sides of her – this he
thinks, is her destiny and glory.*
ELIZABETH BARRETT
Letter to Miss Mitford, February 1845

Terminology was a science she wasn't at all sure of.
She suspected that Robert, more political animal,
proudly bristling his resilient epidermis
would have moved with confidence
at the court of Terminus, rare god of boundaries.
She eyed him cautiously on the other sofa:
yes – cantankerous, but certainly comfortable.
He could parse anything and was a fiend
with crosswords. She sucked her pen thoughtfully
surprising the ailing clockwork in her chest
into another cough. Her lungs
felt like a pair of rotting bellows
in a smithy where the strange conjunction
of heat, flesh, metal, moisture and noise
had made the leather crack unbearably
where the air pressed on the seams.

The Goose and the Gander

*Remember I still enjoin you reading and exercise for the
improvement of your mind and the health of your body, and
grow less romantic, and talk and act like a man of this
world.*
JONATHAN SWIFT,
Letter to Esther Vanhomrigh (Vanessa), 1 June 1722

'The goose and the gander with wave after wave
of honking and cackling seem to chat better
than we two,' thought Robert, on the attack
after a nebulous to and fro all afternoon
about the household finances. 'Why can't I pin her down?
She makes me an ineffectual figure.
I sometimes wish she could immerse herself
in a single task like smoking a cigar
so that I could lean over, tap the leather arm
of her clubbish chair and talk, heart to heart,
man to man.... In fact honking
would be too kind a description of her utterances
– bleating is much nearer the thing.'
Rising, it suddenly occurred to him
that had he dreamt they would become so banal,
he never could have entered on this trip
to market with the silly bleating goose.

Robert and Elizabeth Visit the Norfolk Broads

We differ prodigiously in one point: I fly from the spleen to the world's end, and you run out of your way to meet it.
JONATHAN SWIFT,
Letter to Esther Vanhomrigh (Vanessa), 13 July 1722

At Ranworth we rode into town like a gang;
we had whirled through the lanes for an age
only choosing to stop when we glimpsed
the surprising span of water, fresh through the trees.

He wasn't impressed: his Devon combes and streams
meant beauty. Not this plate of low water
getting gradually dirtied out of existence
by the burgeoning Norfolk mud and weeds.

They didn't sit easily with him, these acres
and acres of confusion between land and water,
with the fenlands sedimenting from open water
through reed fens, swamp carr, wet woodland

to the oaklands of Old England – and not an inch
of sure footage on this raft of putrid stuff.
On Dartmoor he liked the way his footsteps
clicked granite, lifted millions of years ago

from the shallow Devonian seas.
He even thought fondly of Foxtor Mires
where, heading for Childe's Tomb,
our usual route always had us struggling

past bright and bosomy moss cushions
which topped the ooze-filled featherbeds.
The truth is, he just prefers
the way Dartmoor dumps him in the mud.

Robert in the Kitchen in the Dark

Of course these things are not mine. *I think they
are usually spoken of as* ours, *that tea bag of a
word which steeps in the conditional.*
ELIZABETH HARDWICK,
Sleepless Nights

Stepping in here means the end of carpet.
My leading toe locates a tiny lake
next to the sink. At least it *was* my toe
but now I hear and feel a clammy trout
flap sadly in the shallows. Happiness,
I suddenly perceive, is only dry.
My life's a foreign mountain, so uphill,
translating fuzzy shapes into familiars:
I ought to know my teapot, but a scarf
of blurry grey wraps it entirely round.
My memory knows it to be red and slowly,
now I'm staring really hard, I see
faint pink ebb into it and then recede,
a welcome spurt of paint into the dark.
Aboard the drainer, propped in open pose,
the tilted biscuit tin's an obscure helmet,
vague heart for Elizabeth, mucky continent.

Yesterday Was Elizabeth's Turn to Cook

It certainly hasn't the drama of: I saw the old,
white-bearded frigate master on the dock and signed up for
the journey. But after all, 'I' am a woman.
ELIZABETH HARDWICK,
Sleepless Nights

My hair rose a little in the heat
from the lit rings every time
I leaned over the gas. This was
a pose to serve for bowing modestly
to a warm public, but in this setting
more cinematic than theatrical,
framed by the eye level grill just so.
Only chopped onions were in the pan,
the muscles in the face not quite tense,
but not relaxed. The upward movement
of my hair in the heat tickled through
the scalp into the skull and, it seemed,
released the smell of every separate
warmed shaft into the frying air.
I get them mixed up, the warmth
and the heat – and where I feel which:
in my hair, along my arms, at the throat.

Robert Watches Elizabeth Knitting

Knitting is a bore but Elizabeth
nods and smiles and clicks to herself
as though it were more than just useful.
She goes happily about the task,
moving in and out of it without haste,
perfecting tension, cabling, ribs.
She looks forward to the sewing-up
but not too much, knowing how to mesh
the pleasure of the final thing,
all sensuality and wholeness,
with the independent life of every stitch.

Where does it come from, this compulsion
to call her a whole list of things
other than what she is? The string-winder,
the long-fingered, the sitting clock,
the fur-maker and on and on and on.
From shanks by sharp shears to Shape Shoulders
she is what she is, my hank-shifter,
the one who weaves and stitches up wool.

The needles click in a rhythm I can't get at:
part and whole, part and whole;
two heartbeats, a breath, two heartbeats.

Her lips silently move to mark
the four or five last stitches in the line.

Elizabeth's pattern is cut small
and pasted in her diary: a book of days,
a book of stitches; lunch-dates and meetings,
Right Border and Neckband, Left Front.
There is no picture, only the long strings
of phonemes – purls and plains
made unpronounceable by the feminine science
of the knitting pattern. She bows
her head to translate the printed page
into this odd manipulation of sticks and string.

I can't get my mind round knitting.
It starts to have everything
when you come down to it – rhythm,
colour and slow but perceptible change.
The meaning is all in the gaps:
a pattern of holes marked out by woolly colour,
a jumper made of space, division and relations.

Strange to see these youngish hands,
with no puffiness or obvious veins,
repeat the banal and tiny motions
over days over weeks over months.
I ask too much and am too hasty;
this knitting is an exercise in trust.

Robert and Elizabeth Sit Down Again

I was then a 'we'.
ELIZABETH HARDWICK

This was a sudden break from plain routine
as much a surprise as a new baby's strong grasp
or a rake's late notion for the church.
Elizabeth and Robert had not sat down
to write together with the big watch
between them on the deal table,
since that tour of the fells seven years ago
when Robert had been much taken
with a remarkable and fine style of bootrack
which they had chanced on at an inn.
Ah, the heady days, with minds in utter engagement,
mouths distorted in an ache of mutual beaming.
But now this too was important,
new and pleasurable like an unexpected jink
in a straight path, or a glimpse of fresh shade
of pink in a spectrum grown dull.
So much for the sitting down; now for the matter.

PHRASE BOOK

Only the poor cells cannot comment.

MIROSLAV HOLUB,
The Dimension of the Present Moment and Other Essays

Tom and Jerry Visit England

O boy, I thought. A chance
to visit England and O boy here, out
of nowhere, a voice to describe it. Reader,
I dreamt of coming back to tell you how I marched
round the Tower of London, in a beefeater suit,
swished my axe at Jerry, belted after him
into the Bloody Tower, my back legs
circling like windmills in a gale
while ravens flapped around our heads.
You would hear it all: tea with the Queen
at Buckingham Palace and me scattering
the cucumber sandwiches at the sight
of Jerry by the silver salver. I couldn't wait
for the gorgeous tableau: Queenie with her mouth
in a little shocked screaming shape, her crown
gone crooked as she stood cringing on the throne
with her skirts up round her knees, and Jerry
down there laughing by the footstool.
I would be a concertina zig-zag by that time
with a bone china cup stuffed in my face
and a floral tea pot shoved on my head so hard
my brains would form a spout and a handle
when it cracked and dropped off.

I can't get this new voice to explain to you
the ecstasy in the body when you fling
yourself into such mayhem, open yourself
to any shape at all and able to throw out
stars of pain for everyone to see.

But reader, the visit wasn't like that.
I ended up in a poem and it made me uneasy.
Cats prefer to skulk and sulk
in the dark, we prefer mystery
and slinking. This is even true of me
with my stupid human face opening
into only two or three stupid expressions:
cunning, surprise and maybe rage.
And I couldn't find Jerry.
'Where's the mouse?' I tripped
over commas and colons hard like diamonds, looking
for him. 'Where's the mouse?' I kept asking,
'Where's the mouse?' I banged full face into a query –
and ended up with my front shaped
like a question mark for hours. That was scary:
I usually pop right back into myself in seconds.
So I hesitated for once before flinging myself
down the bumpy staircase where all the lines ended.
I went on my rear and at the bottom you would have seen me,
end up, bristling with splinters, and nose down
snuffling for any trace of mouse smell.
Reader, it was my first tragic movie:
I couldn't find the mouse.

Pavlova's Physics

Everything in my body
has been processed
through at least one star
(except for the hydrogen).

I want to speak to you about it;
I want you to know how much
I understand – and more and more
reveals itself in waves.

I'm really a wise kid,
the kind that gets on and doesn't
need to go to college to do it,
secretly learning to peel back

the potent leaves of mathematics
while boning up on Greek at night.
For all that, the consciousness
is an outdated barn of a thing,

a slow phenomenon compared
to the speed of the senses.
Today even I'm entranced
by the marine symmetry of my body

but, believe me, this world
is a place of bizarre consequences
where matter can appear
out of nothing and where

the light of stars is ancient
history when it gets here:
we can never understand
what we're living through at the time.

You can show me your piece of warm
thigh the length of Florida
and I'm telling you, I'm affected
by the way you look at me but I need

more dimensions than geography allows.
I'm falling forward, tumbling
into increasing disorder; yes, disorder
is increasing in the universe

and will keep increasing until
the whole shebang becomes a place
where it is remembered
only the alert rodents swam.

Brando on Commuting

It's the knees you notice
on everyone except yourself, but
when you're sitting down you
can't help staring
at the more personal zones
though people blockade them
with what they can: papers,
briefcases, macs. We approach
the lights of the next platform
as tenderly as the big ship
noses the quay.

You think of sex on the tube,
a lot, and you can see the others
do too: nurse lies on a bed
strewn with important documents
her white uniform bunched
round her waist, the papers
sticky and crinkled underneath.
You can't really see the bodies
in the moonlight. Gauguin

and Ligeti are on in London
say the posters across
the track. I like a woman
who understands Gauguin
and Ligeti and I like her
in silk, a vision
sent to me through the grime.

She will be cool, from
a family with a company
about to fly like pirates
on the stock markets
of the world. We'll swim

naked and touch
underwater for what
seems like a year
until I cut through
her shyness like a crusader.

In the heat of the underground
among the rainbow lines
the trains nuzzle the platforms
like fish. They are deaf
and their lives are quiet
and glorious as they take
up and disgorge the litter
of people all along
the flexible length of their bodies.
They run to the cardinal points

of the system: photography
can't snap them in the tunnels
as they crisscross and interweave,
playing like marine mammals.
I think they do the works
down here, present themselves
in courtship colours, each
segment gleaming like ice.

How exactly one services another,
how the glass walls of their sides
stay intact, how they

are prevented from flying
off with their lovers –
if they are prevented,
we could be going anywhere,
for all I know – you just can't tell.
This thing could have sails, or wings
as it commutes, we commute,
I commute, finally rising
away from the scene
on a moving staircase, rising
and admiring the poster art
as I go.

Superman Sounds Depressed

Nothing could have prepared me for this life
in which it all hinges on me,

where it's only me and my past now left
to reassure the world. The trouble is

they forget me fast and start counting
on krill, or thinking they understand

turbulence: so I have to make regular
appearances on the borders

of disaster, dropping through some backdoor
in space whenever I feel the gravity

of their need. Apples for the teacher
are all I get for it, for holding the railway

train on the high viaduct by a single joint
of my little finger, for blowing hard

at the last moment to keep the water upright
in the shape of the shattered dam, for stopping

a model of the earth based on real chaos from
breaking through. I feel spelled all wrong,

stuck in the east wind
with my face caught in an expression

which would mean world financial crisis
if the president wore it. Give me dinner,

a lovely long dinner in dim light, with someone,
someone who will propose something rude

so it doesn't sound rude – just delicious –
nothing personal, anxious or brutal about it

though it might seem all of those things
to others when it's not night, over their ordinary

sandwiches: wholemeal, mustard
and fragile morsels. My head aches; I want

that woman and enough passion to blast away
any hope of understanding what's happening

to me. And I want us to eat scallops,
and I want to lick the juice from her chin

as though I could save the world that way,
and I won't even ask what passion is for.

Goat

Dusk, deserted road, and suddenly
I was a goat. To be truthful, it took
two minutes, though it seemed sudden,
for the horns to pop out of my skull,
for the spine to revolutionise and go
horizontal, for the fingers to glue
together and for the nails to become
important enough to upgrade to hoof.
The road was not deserted any more, but full
of goats, and I liked that, even though I hate
the rush hour on the tube, the press of bodies.
Now I loved snuffling behind his or her ear,
licking a flank or two, licking and snuffling here,
there, wherever I liked. I lived for the push
of goat muscle and goat bone, the smell of goat fur,
goat breath and goat sex. I ended up on the edge
of the crowd where the road met the high
hedgerow with the scent of earth, a thousand
kinds of grass, leaves and twigs, flower-heads
and the intoxicating tang of the odd ring-pull
or rubber to spice the mixture. I wanted
to eat everything. I could have eaten the world
and closed my eyes to nibble at the high
sweet leaves against the sunset. I tasted
that old sun and the few dark clouds
and some tall buildings far away in the next town.
I think I must have swallowed an office block
because this grinding enormous digestion tells me
it's stuck on an empty corridor which has
at the far end, I know, a tiny human figure.

Love Song with a Flock of Sheep

'Win a flock of sheep' said the advertisement.
'Sheep Dip: an eight year old pure malt whisky.
You will find an entry form on every bottle.'

I will. I will buy the whisky,
I will find the entry form. I will:
I will win the sheep and I'll give them to you.

Keep the flock at home
and let them graze around the house.
Kindly and damp, they'll eat the carpet
and will start on the wallpaper too;
your interior decorations will be masticated away.
The flock is softer than soft furnishings
but when they've eaten all that they'll start
on the hard stuff. They'll munch their way
through the mantelpiece and everything –
your books, your manuscripts –
will fly into their placid mouths.

I know you. You'll like it better without
all that ruminated stuff. You want
the woolly life, carding and spinning,
with only sheep for furniture and bedclothes.
The flock will find you out eventually
and start their blowing in your ears
and their nuzzling across your hair.
It will begin in the kitchen with a fleecy
brush along the backs of your knees.
They'll surround you on the sofa
and drink out of your bath. Your clothes

will go into the three stomachs and in the dark
you'll feel sheep nibble between your toes
and suck your toenails. They will graze
your legs, removing every hair with teeth
so precise and shy you'll feel only
a mist of breath and lips. They'll move
in a cloud across your chest, your belly,
face and beard – everywhere – cropped
down to a downy stubble, peaceful as pasture.
Soon you will be as shorn as a yearling lamb
and twice as happy, blissoming with the flock.

When I arrive, dressed as Bo-Peep,
I won't get a look in. But by hook or by crook
you shall have them anyway: sheep fleecy, sheep shorn
and me lovelorn.

Vegetable Love

I'd like to say the fridge
was clean, but look at the rusty
streaks down the back wall
and the dusty brown pools
underneath the salad crisper.

And this is where I've lived
the past two weeks, since I was pulled
from the vegetable garden.
I'm wild for him: I want to stay crunchy
enough to madden his hard palate and his tongue,
every sensitive part inside his mouth.
But almost hour by hour now, it seems,
I can feel my outer leaves losing resistance,
as oxygen leaks in, water leaks out
and the same tendency creeps further
and further towards my heart.

Down here there's not much action,
just me and another, even limper, lettuce
and half an onion. The door opens so many,
so many times a day but he never looks
in the salad drawer where I'm curled in a corner.

There's an awful lot of meat. Strange cuts:
whole limbs with their grubby hair,
wings and thighs of large birds,
claws and beaks. New juice
gathers pungency as it rolls down
through the smelly strata of the refrigerator,
and drips on to our fading heads.

The thermostat is kept as low as it will go,
and when the weather changes
for the worse, what's nearest
to the bottom of the fridge starts to freeze.
Three times we've had cold snaps,
and I've felt the terrifying pain
as ice crystals formed at my fringes.

Insulation isn't everything in here:
you've got to relax into the cold,
let it in at every pore. It's proper
for food preservation. But I heat up
again at the thought of him,
at the thought of mixing into one juice
with his saliva, of passing down his throat
and being ingested with the rest
into his body cells where I'll learn
by osmosis another lovely version
of curl, then shrivel, then open again to desire.

I'm Contemplated by a Portrait of a Divine

I cannot speak to you. My lips are fused
where an archangel kissed them. I have never
made much of myself although I know,
sometimes, that space is touching me
because I have seen the crack in the universe
through which the galaxies stream. O God,
I will always know how to walk, no rest, until
it just ends in blackness when I fall down flat.
I have one arching eyebrow: my whole life
is in that eyebrow where an angel nestles
at the root of every hair, raising it up.
Dear Christ, I can hear vice rushing through
the grass. There is someone here.
If I could lick the glass
clean from this side, I might see her, though
I already know she would look the way
I want my soul to look. This pose
which I strain to keep, in which I lean
on the desk for dear life, is not a pose.
It's so important for keeping the drawer shut
in case my heart should slip out, fly up.

Leonardo and the Vortex

I get like him sometimes:
seeing the same shape in everything
I look at, the same tones
in everything I hear.

But I'll never make a deluge drawing
or be gripped by the science of circular
motion. And I probably won't learn to care how
many complex collisions happen in a pool
when water is trickled from above.
How currents percuss against each other,
and how waves rebound into the air, falling
again to splash up more water in smaller
and smaller versions of the same.
How a storm is different where air and water mix,
bursting again and again through the thin skin
which separates them. How a woman's hair
moves in spouts and spirals just like water
and how the leaves of the star plant
trail on the ground in a loose coil.
And look at your sleeve, folding and swirling
around your arm, and the pattern of fine black hairs
curving from inner wrist to outer elbow,
and the underlying muscles relying on that slight
twist around the lower arm for their strength,
and the blood coiling around your body
through the little eddies in the larger veins
and arteries, coiling towards the vortex
in the chambers of your heart where I sit,
where the impetus has pulled me in.

Her Lover's Ear

I woke up as a flying speck in the sunshine
which bothered me for a while, because I missed you,
though whirling in the air was a thrill.
I zoomed along the breeze tracks,
learning to accelerate into gravity,
floating up at the last by hitching
on to a draught from the door crack.
But nobody notices a mote, so, bored,
I moved into calmer air. Even here
there were surges and lulls which
buffeted me around – waves
rocking me towards your ear.

Everywhere on the body, touch makes sound
but the ear is the one place
you can't tell them apart,
where even the noise of a fingertip
rustles and explodes.

I was glad to see you:
I thought I might know in my human life
how to touch you lightly
after this rehearsal as a piece of dust.

I tripped against your lobe
just so you would know I was there,
and felt the fine hairs rise in the notch above.
As the air pushed me round the helix,
I leaned outwards on the bend like a biker
so I could press against the rim
in a long brush as the air flowed past

just gritty enough for you to feel.
Swept into the bowl of the concha
I felt you move as I tickled against
your skin and skidded softly
with the momentum into your skull.

Matter

He touched my skin
all afternoon
as though he could feel
the smallest particles
which make me up.

By tea time he knew each
of the billions of electrons
which fly through my body
every second.

Then I think he was searching
for the particles
not yet discovered
but believed to exist.

Then I didn't know
what time it was any more
and neither of us knew
which was inside or outside
as he reached somewhere
very deep and fingered gold –
charms, stranges, tops and gravitons –
but not the words he wanted
which only come now.

Muse

When I kiss you in all the folding places
of your body, you make that noise like a dog
dreaming, dreaming of the long run he makes
in answer to some jolt to his hormones,
running across landfills, running, running
by tips and shorelines from the scent of too much,
but still going with head up and snout
in the air because he loves it all
and has to get away. I have to kiss deeper
and more slowly – your neck, your inner arm,
the neat creases under your toes, the shadow
behind your knee, the white angles of your groin –
until you fall quiet because only then
can I get the damned words to come into my mouth.

The Room

She gives a fingernail clipping
to the naked man.
It will fly up
and amaze him
when she's gone.

He balances it
on his belly:
it's light and dry.

The noisy thing.
He is sure
he can hear
it speaking
as he grazes
it softly all over
his skin.

On Tour: The Alps

But today the sun shines as we arrive
at the highest point, and my bloke's grumbling
that a pass is a strange place to stop. No one
else sleeps over he says – other tourists pause

for a beer, a photograph or two and head on,
to Italy the one way, to Switzerland the other.
Only hikers and a smattering of soldiers
have made up reasons to stay. Ah. Breathe.

Ignore him. We're at the very heart of Europe,
a place where everyone's a traveller, moving: last century
Byron passed in his rattling coach, purpose-built
for European tours. I imagine its special

fittings, pure James Bond: the walls
inside are soft, padded velvet, crimson and you
sink into the seats so it's difficult to get up.
They are slightly too narrow and the coach's sway

round Alpine hairpins pitches you against
your neighbour's shoulder or if things are really going
his way, into his lap. Does a cabinet of drinks
swing out of the mahogany panel? Do the seats

collapse at the touch of a button to throw you
wriggling on your back? The carriage rollocks
along, mountain scenery passes in a blur
and I'm falling for Byron's smile, his charming

weaknesses, his warm coach, the springs
squeaking and bouncing, horses'
breath steaming away into the mountain night fog.
There's enough madness in me to fall,

enough to spare for a smile as the carriage
slows and I'm flung out at dawn,
dumped on my rear by a roadside
in the Alpine foothills, Italy or Switzerland,

or some other country where no one speaks
a language I know, and the back of the coach lurches
round curves into the distance where
I can hear, I think, the amazing tang of cowbells.

⌇

Could be I'm just remembering it from higher up
where, let's all come down to earth, I really am.
Breathe in, yes, our party's at the top of the pass,
and listen, amidst the true sound of cowbells,

the tourists, the climbers, the smattering of soldiers.
We're guided here by my lover's bad temper,
and my panic to settle him in an astonishing spot
because there's all Europe to pick on, and we

desperately want to get him peachy again,
to get the mean spider out of his brain where
it's sat all day, spoiling. And I feel
responsible: it's my continent on show.

We climbed here in a Volvo but the mountain museum
tells us Wordsworth walked all the way, proud
to be pedestrian. I could have done that too,
could have matched him step for step

even in the snow. Everywhere a new pathway,
and I'm there with him, to help turn walking
into statement, more than just somewhere to go. We talk
politics as much as topography and I help him

by thinking legs, not imagination
so we can do thirty, sometimes more miles
a day, even in this mountain territory.
I watch him stride off-scene towards

imagined terrible peaks, leaving me
a scrap of local colour in the dark, set
against herds you can't see but hear
in soft clangs as they move through the mist.

∽

The inn's homely, smells of wood and climbers'
leather, canvas; my lover's pleased that beer
and wurst is generous, cheap. Note the tremendous
view across the pass from our room, only

the evening fog's come down with a vengeance
and we're sitting in thick cloud. The walls
are dark pine and the ceiling painted
with animals, ladies, lovely scenes you want to be in,

in a way, but not so tied down. Later, in the bar,
the receptionist stares at my lover while
she whispers to me in German about Goethe,
how he stayed here for his geology

to make a study of the mountain stones.
Sweet Goethe, picking among the minerals –
I could spot them just as smartly, find
something precious for his delectation,

chuckle as he rolls little boulders towards
my feet, piles them between my legs. Look at me
supervising sacks of rocks, naming and weighing
just like him, testing and cataloguing too.

∽

The bed's huge, the way around it tight.
We have to make complicated choices,
who's to get in, out: one of us is always in the way.
High off the ground, too, that bed, a real clamber

and all night a background fear of the drop to the floor.
The room, the bed, the cloud, the view, give my lover
dreams until dawn. For hours he mutters and groans
a stack of nouns – names of stars, of women, of things

in the world outside our wooden box. And the room starts
to lose its charm for me as my mind too drifts
outside towards the dark up there somewhere
above the mountain fog, towards the muffled stars.

Beneath the quilt, a mountain in itself,
I'm wondering, as I reach to comfort him,
about love – how it lets in the whole world,
even the cloud sitting on the mountain top,

the awfulness of the stars we can't see,
the animals, walkers, cars rolling
across the pass, the very dark itself and
I want it to be daytime, I badly want not to listen

to him shouting now in his dreams he's had
enough, calling out names I don't know. I want to jump
into the car and coast him down to the lakes,
where it will be different and in the mornings

I can bring fresh raspberries from the market.
And we do leave, after breakfast, we do,
but even as far as Lucerne I'm listening
for the strange clang that tells you

mountain animals are on the move
only it's hard to tune my ear to it
against so many men's voices shouting
all the names they know, at the dark.

Phrase Book

I'm standing here inside my skin,
which will do for a Human Remains Pouch
for the moment. Look down there (up here).
Quickly. Slowly. This is my own front room

where I'm lost in the action, live from a war,
on screen. I am an Englishwoman, I don't understand you.
What's the matter? You are right. You are wrong.
Things are going well (badly). Am I disturbing you?

TV is showing bliss as taught to pilots:
Blend, Low silhouette, Irregular shape, Small,
Secluded. (Please write it down. Please speak slowly.)
Bliss is how it was in this very room

when I raised my body to his mouth,
when he even balanced me in the air,
or at least I thought so and yes the pilots say
yes they have caught it through the Side-Looking

Airborne Radar, and through the J-Stars.
I am expecting a gentleman (a young gentleman,
two gentlemen, some gentlemen). Please send him
(them) up at once. This is really beautiful.

Yes they have seen us, the pilots, in the Kill Box
on their screens, and played the routine for
getting us Stealthed, that is, Cleansed, to you and me,
Taken Out. They know how to move into a single room

like that, to send in with Pinpoint Accuracy, a hundred Harms.
I have two cases and a cardboard box. There is another
bag there. I cannot open my case – look out,
the lock is broken. Have I done enough?

Bliss, the pilots say, is for evasion
and escape. What's love in all this debris?
Just one person pounding another into dust,
into dust. I do not know the word for it yet.

Where is the British Consulate? Please explain.
What does it mean? What must I do? Where
can I find? What have I done? I have done
nothing. Let me pass please. I am an Englishwoman.

In the Bath

She was interested in prehistory.
It didn't seem so long ago and offered
pleasant notions of a time before civic duty,
when disease was accepted and fought through,
or not. Hers wasn't a museum interest:
it was as tight, neat and uncomplicated
as a reef knot. 'If I came here as a visitor
from Mars, I would be impressed by the water,
the relative health of the inhabitants, the indecent
urge of atoms for complexity – they don't just split
once, think they're clever, and then stop.' She imagined
her body cells spreading like a film to cover the earth,
coating every frond in the tropical rain forest,
every blade of grass on the pampas. Herself
spread thin and making the surface of the world
sparkle. It was a stunning vision of the future.
She lay in the bath with the water touching
her all over, and remembered that not even
the most tender lover could do that. She wondered
if every molecule on the surface of her skin
was wet and what wet meant to such very
tiny matter. To make things worse, or at least
more difficult for the water, she raised her body
slightly, building an island chain of hip bones,
belly, breasts all of which began to dry at once.
She loved the water trails over her body curves,
the classical lines between wet and dry
making graph patterns which she thought might follow

the activity in her brain – all she wanted
was to be a good atlas, a bright school map
to shine up the world for everyone to see.

The Mad Cow Talks Back

I'm not mad. It just seems that way
because I stagger and get a bit irritable.
There are wonderful holes in my brain
through which ideas from outside can travel
at top speed and through which voices,
sometimes whole people, speak to me
about the universe. Most brains are too
compressed. You need this spongy
generosity to let the others in.

I love the staggers. Suddenly the surface
of the world is ice and I'm a magnificent
skater turning and spinning across whole hard
Pacifics and Atlantics. It's risky when
you're good, so of course the legs go before,
behind, and to the side of the body from time
to time, and then there's the general embarrassing
collapse, but when that happens it's glorious
because it's always when you're travelling
most furiously in your mind. My brain's like
the hive: constant little murmurs from its cells
saying this is the way, this is the way to go.

Shopping

I approved of it heartily, the multiway underwired bra
from the Pearls Collection in lots of nonstandard sizes.
I took it to try. Next groceries, and maybe a plant or two,
something green and exotic enough to refresh my system,
to help me imagine the place off-shore
where I recently stashed my savings. You could
exchange it too, the multiway bra, if it didn't fit:
a serious life or time consideration. I am mostly
vegetarian and skitter up the supermarket aisles
pursuing my health. What goes in that basket is important.
I like it to be from the country, something that had a green
and happy life once, that knew hope and had a generous
and juicy nature. You can't make deals with your stomach
about the future. I try to avoid this craze and that craze
but if you're going to delay death and stay in your prime
week in week out you have to make the hard choices
of the supermarket. Salivating over the loin chops
in the freezer and still passing by equates with goodness
or at least good sense which is the nearest we can get to it
at this time, halving the odds on immediate decay, keeping
a firm straight back well into middle age, the signal
that you want something badly or want something badly not
to happen, because should it happen you're never ready
these days, days of oils, marks and time.

The Mad Cow in Love

I want to be an angel and really think
I'm getting there with this mind of mine,
shrinking every day towards the cleanness,
the size of a baby animal's brain.
Trouble is, I want you to be an angel too
– and want that more if anything. It's one
of those demands I can't raise just like that,
evenings, when we're reading our different newspapers
you scanning your pages and me mine for an item
to start speech, make mouths smile, knees touch – something
in all that murder and mayhem to launch love.
You tell me you're looking for news of the self.
Do you want to be an angel? I know
the answer already and it's rough medicine.
But think of all the kinds there are, as many
as the different degrees of reaching
for the good. You might get away without
searching for the soul at all in those places,
today at least, you'd rather not get to know.
And angels do a variety of jobs:
the post of perpetual adoration might suit,
or divine messenger but I fancy for you
the government of the stars and all the elements.
I know you well enough to choose, after all this time
as foreign correspondent on the track of who you are,
looking for leads: your last screw, the food
you threw away, your strategic approaches
for living through the next hour. I don't mean it,
though, any of it. I want you earthly,

including all the global terrors and harms
which might come when we fall backwards
into the world of horn and hoof.

Mad Cow Dance

I like to dance. Bang. I love to dance. Push.

It makes me savage and brilliant. Stomp. To
my own rhythm, rhythm. I lead or I don't

have a partner. No market for partners,
just this wide floor for the dance.
I think I was born here. Swoop. I don't care.

Even if I'd been born in the back of a car

the chassis and each blessed spring
would have jumped as I leapt out

of my mum. Up. Down to the ocean, perhaps
the beach? Hah. Stone steps and stone walls,
the pebbled strand, try to stall my special

high-kicks for the sea. But fireflies

know I'm here, raving with light,
they swirl down my spine. Swish. My tail

goes bam, thwack against the backs
of my legs. Pleasure, local pleasure.
Listen, sitting-down reader, I reckon

faces would be red if you knew what

was next. The little fibres
of my muscles give me such a charge.

Bread and butter. Release. Ceasefire
between my legs and my brain. Sweet oil
flows down to my little hooves. I like

to turn and call to my friends in

northern towns: kick out, kick back, fruity,
for a second. We can meet among characters

who don't dance, and hoof it till dawn, gas
on and on even when we're moving the most.
Four legs increase splits into splats,

just watch me

become
pure product, pure

use,
pure perfume,
jasmine and fucked.

Volumes

They put me in a fever. It's not enough
to look. I want to hold them all
and stuff them in the gaps in my head.
I gallop past Health towards Travel
where I break into a muck sweat
as I lift and sniff a book about Verona.
The odour makes me stagger and long
to be a book mite, to live right inside
and gulp holes through the picture maps.
I don't trust myself in Fiction. The thought
of those thousands and thousands of stories —
the crush and babble of other minds —
makes the whites of my eyes show and roll.
Last time I sauntered by those shelves
I slammed into the New Titles display
and crashed right through a pyramid of books
on to my back among the toppled photos
of authors winking at the carry on.
I got a cuppa and a pat on the rump
from the kind saleslady who has the bubble
of book hysteria herself, I'd guess.
If she could, she'd wear print on her skin.
There are words written for everything,
I think, and it's only a matter of time
before I find a new 'How To' book:
how to stand upright, how not to fall
and how not to cry out when you do.

The Mad Cow Tries to Write the Good Poem

The police came once when I was doing my death dance
to the amazing circular music which had entered a gap
near my cortex and acted as powerfully as a screwdriver
on my soul. I wove in and out of the green trees. I used
my hooves as gentle weapons in the air. A bit of newspaper
fame came my way that day, but shit, it was a performance,
ephemeral, and certainly not the good poem. Lasting.
How can I last when I live in a shed and even
the postman doesn't know how to find me?
It's dark in here. Light would echo the gaps
in my brain coils and set off a fizzing reaction,
not so much pounding, more an explosion
followed by a flowing moment when the taboo
people arrive. They're dressed in red and
stand formally around my skull as though staged
for an opera. And when they sing – sometimes as many
as seven at once – then, friend, please, the good
poem is sounding all round this hut, my head, the world,
I hear it written in the streaky emulsion on the walls,
in my own messing on the floor, in the nation's smeary dailies,
in lovely people's ears, their breath, your breath:
it's new every time, always wanted and easy to spot
because I know what it looks like with my eyes closed.

A Walk in the Snow

There's something shameless about
snowfall, the way it lies there,
does nothing but changes everything.
So when freak storms hit London

I couldn't resist all that cleanness;
the glitter on the street outside
made me salivate, the dazzle
and glamour on our ordinary road.

I tottered out with Deirdre, sliding –
sliding worst of all where ice
was topped by snow. We hung on
to each other. I don't know who hung

more or hung on longer, while we rocked
with laughter and those sharp movements
the upper body makes to stay upright.
Breathless like that you talk too loudly,

as though the volume's been turned right up.
Everything's big – the rhythm of your body
too large, too loud in the effort to keep
your torso pointed straight down the pavement,

your legs true to where you want to go.
We were heading for the park, and we made it,
but left ourselves too tired even to think
about the end. The helpless feeling made us laugh

until I fell on my back in the snow,
my breath, the laughter and the cold air
bursting in my chest as I lay there.
Sick, dizzy and squinting in the sunshine

I looked up to see a spread of branches
filled with frost, every twig cluttered
with wings, haloes, stars. Deirdre
plonked herself next to me and, of course,

after we'd sat there we couldn't get up.
We had to roll over and over towards
the nearest tree, crawling the last part.
A stupid dog, the small sort, found us

and jumped and snuffled and yapped until I said,
'If the fucker would shut up, everybody
wouldn't see us.' We edged close enough
to the tree for Deirdre to pull herself up,

then she reached out for me. We were laughing
so hard water was running down our legs and I said,
'Deirdre, did you ever think we would come to this?'
And she said, 'No, never, never, never.'

The Mad Cow Believes She is the Spirit of the Weather

People out walking lean into the wind, the rain:
they believe it thwarts the weather to welcome it like that.
I can happily get lost for hours in a swirl of showers
because I was born into weather. They still tell
how my mother pushed me out of her body
on to a rock and I split the stone in two while the rain
washed me and the thunder broke overhead.
I was a junior cloud goddess, with storms following
me, winds and whirlwinds, shots of rain
and a split sky above my head. Always moving,
I kept one jump ahead of getting wet, kicking
back at the clouds with my hind legs
to keep them there. It's harder now, here
in the future: my brain has the characteristics
of a sponge and the rain seeps into the holes.
I think I'm making chaos. My vests
don't keep me warm and when I last sneezed
a volcano in the Pacific threw a sheet of dust
around the world. I'm dangerous to the earth.
I spat and a blanket of algae four miles long
bloomed on the Cornish coast. I rubbed
the sleep from my eyes and a meteor large enough
to make the earth wobble in its orbit
came very close indeed. I have been sad recently
and now the weather has changed for good.

Work in the City

Yes I do hold down a job and I find
the air in my brain helps combat
the stress. Once, carrying
my lunch back to the office, the tea
steaming in a polystyrene cup, the roll crunched
in a paper bag under my arm, the juggle
of food, briefcase, drink started to collapse.
It was around midday. I know the commuter
paths from the station, how to weave through
the concrete walkways, over roads in the spots
where traffic parts and lets you miraculously
through. These are the routes where the classic
people live, the ones who'll stick in my memory cells
even when the mind's shot, great blank slots of time
and visions revolving by turns like the movies.
They are the ones who ask me for everything
as I go by, every day, everything I have. One boy
leans against the wood palings he sleeps behind,
calling for change from his nest of blankets,
calling for my cup of tea, calling me love
as he crawls through the gap in the wood.
It's hard to stay perfect on that route, but
this day I was smiling at a lovely fantasy
until I slipped up on a piece of hamburger mashed
on the road, turning the juggle with my possessions
into a full stunt routine, legs, arms flying, the food
I was bound to waste at the end of it all. Then
the boy with the mad embroidery of muck
on his lapel stared me down again, daring me
to be bad. I offered him my apple and he turned

green, muttered, clasped his body in many places
and swung away. I sensed I was getting a tongue-lashing
and didn't want to ignore it, but I couldn't understand
a word. I put the food in a little pile in front of him,
the steaming tea, the papers, briefcase, all
the bags. I took off my coat, my shoes, every
piece of clothing and stood sweating in the light rain
but he didn't want me to know his language,
his eminence, his damnation or his delight.

MY LIFE ASLEEP

What are all those
fuzzy-looking things out there?
WILLIAM CARLOS WILLIAMS

Thetis

No man can frighten me. Watch as I stretch
my limbs for the transformation, I'm laughing
to feel the surge of other shapes beneath my skin.
It's like this: here comes the full thrill of my art
as the picture of a variegated
lizard insinuates itself into my mind.
I extend my neck, lengthen fingers, push
down toes to find the form. My back begins
to undulate, the skin to gleam. I think
my soul has slithered with me into this
shape as real as the little, long tongue in my mouth,
as the sun on my back, as the skill in absolute stillness.
My name is Thetis Creatrix and you,
voyeur, if you looked a little closer, would see
the next ripples spread up my bloody tail, to bloom
through my spine as the bark begins to harden
over my trunk. Already I'm so much the oak
I lean everything towards the black oxygen
in the black air, I process delicious gases
through my personal chemistry, suck moisture
from the earth to a pulse so slow you can't detect it.
Next tigress. Low tremendous purrs start at the pit
of my stomach, I'm curving through long grass,
all sinew, in a body where tension
is the special joy and where the half-second
before a leap tells it all. Put out a paw
to dab a stone, an ant, a dead lamb. Life,
my life, is all play even up to the moment

when I'm tripped up, thrown down, bound,
raped until I bleed from my eyes,
beaten out of shape and forced to bring forth War.

Thetis was a sea goddess who had the marvellous ability to change her shape. Peleus was taught by Proteus the way to overcome her: to bind her and hold on tightly whatever shape she took. The result of this forced union was Achilles.

The Swallows Move In

You, with the new haircut, steadily
scrape birdshit from the sink and from
the rusty washing machine, because
swallows are nesting in your outhouse

and mustn't be disturbed. Didn't you notice
lightning shake the wires where the birds
perch at dusk? While you scrub the smelly drainer
and prod at dung in the bowl, the city shakes

with news from Europe, with news of the minister
and the actress, with news of the prince
and the married woman. Houses subside
all over London, and a taxi-driver swore

he'd seen medieval apprentices skating
on frozen Moorfields with bones of animals
tied to their shoes to swirl them across the ice.
You patiently lay old papers for protection

across the lawnmower and the bicycle,
the sink and the sad spin-dryer. A crumb
of shit is in your eye but you try to wink
back at the newspaper photographs of ministers,

married women, murdered women, refugees,
the mauled and mutilated of the world,
the weeping dead themselves, photographs
which make you wonder how a person

could look at that and not die of shame,
the same photos you are spreading
with care against the dirt of swallows who play
and swoop at midges in the light summer air.

War and Peace

The woods of Normandy are hot with stars
underfoot, resistance and memory.
It's the Queen's birthday and we know the stars
are flowers in reality because
today flowers are everywhere for her.
Yellow smoke hangs over the bridge
at Mostar and someone has taken
huge bites out of the town, chewed up
apartment blocks. Yes, it's peacetime.
Grab your shopping trolley at Tesco's
and read the sign: *DO NOT HESITATE*

WHEN PASSING THROUGH THIS GATE
and you don't, you don't hesitate
knowing you're about to buy a world
in the supermarket someone else
lost recently. Peacetime. Here is Mostar
still dressed in yellow smoke. The Queen
marks her anniversary by doing a bungee jump
at Crystal Palace, a two-hundred feet plunge,
in full regalia. She yo-yos up and down
as her tiara crashes to the ground.
Meanwhile, behind the roof of the château

yellow clouds rise where windows, even frames
blow out; the works of art are moved elsewhere.
The problem is not living together, pulling together,
the problem is dying. A little boat
leaves the bridge at Mostar and shudders
towards the white mists of Niagara,
whose plunge and roar is thrilling all the tourists.

Peace. The engines grind against the undertow
as the captain takes us as far into the mist
and thunder as he thinks we dare to go.

'Delectable Creatures'

You won't remember, but it was
October and the street trees
still coloured like rude bouquets.
I had some rare walks by the river,
the weak sun loose on the water
and the light so washed out and lovely
it would make you cry if you weren't
completely alert. Every step I took
they were uncovering something: people
sleeping under cardboard, a lost riverboat
marooned on a freak low tide, the buried flotsam
which made metal detectors buzz, theatres
with resonant names: the Rose, the Globe.

And I was carrying a torch for someone
to the point of hallucination:
we rolled in flames through seven fields, the burning
so thorough I longed to be shocked by water,
a faceful of anything, even the smelly Thames.

And I remember the press full of doctors,
of inventions; a herringbone fragment
of DNA to fool a virus, a wisp
of vitamin to lock on to inner decay
and knock it dead for good. We were
saving vouchers, too, for air miles.

There was, O yes, the morning I woke up
to see an open book, drying on the drainer.
Dimly reconstructing the night before
I remembered dropping off, head on the desk,

getting up moments later, to select the book
with extra-exquisite care from any old shelf.
I slowly chose a page, spread it with jam
and butter, and tried to stuff it down my mouth.
It was, of course, Freud's *Jokes and the Unconscious*.
I must have tried to wash it like a tea plate,
stacked it, then put myself into my bed.

I think the explanation could be this:
that in the light, the river was sometimes pink,
and St Paul's was pink, and even Lloyd's
in the distance was pink, as I crossed Waterloo Bridge
with a purchase under my arm, some piece
of frou frou or a novel to bring me back
from the seven fields, back to the river-mist
which must once have been river water, back
to breathing mist so deeply I could feel
each droplet hit my diaphragm like shot.

Quark

'Transcendental,' said the technician,
'to stumble on a quark that talks back.
I will become a mystagogue, initiate
punters into the wonder of it for cash.'
'Bollocks,' said the quark, from its aluminium
nacelle. 'I don't need no dodgy
crypto-human strategising my future.
Gonna down-size under the cocoplum
or champak, drink blue marimbas into
the sunset, and play with speaking quarklike
while I beflower the passing gravitons.'

The Alchemist

I've waited my whole life for these few atoms
to swim, synchronised, into tetrahedra
(that's diamonds to you, sunshine, crystal gold).
But it all goes pear-shaped or, at least, cuboid,
so I end up with pyrites or galenae
or magnificent prisms of boring, boring quartz.
But you, my auriferous lovely, have just to breathe
and mica condenses in the very air.
I'm the acolyte of your reticulations,
a zealot for your mineral ideology.

My Life Asleep

Everything is loud: the rasp of bed-sheets,
clamour of hair-tangles, clink of teeth.
Small sweat takes up residence in each crease
of the body, but breathing's even, herself warm,
room safe as a London room can be.
The tube rumbles only metres underneath
and planes for Heathrow circle on the roof.
You'll find the body and all the air it exhales
smellier than by day; she's kinder, more supple.
Bend close to catch the delicacies of sleep,
to hear skin tick, to taste the mandragora
of night sweat. Lean forward and put a finger
on the spot you think the dream is.

Noah's Dove

It seemed the end of drizzling. Doves pair for life:
a tidy species to invite into the ark.
Men have no wings, no, not even Noah

so when the rain stopped he sought out the birds.
An old raven went first, wheeled around the dark sky
half the day just for kicks. He looped the loop, then hid

behind a cloud, only to return with no damned news
at all. A dove stops searching once she's felt the beak
of her first mate in the soft feathers of her neck.

Hopeless at distances, not used to questing,
she was sent out next, after the raven,
on the mission of her life. She went three times

the last time for good, en route to her own rainbow.
She left her mate the only single soul aboard,
trying to think of ways to spawn himself.

Mrs Noah: Taken after the Flood

I can't sit still these days. The ocean
is only memory, and my memory as fluttery
as a lost dove. Now the real sea beats
inside me, here, where I'd press fur and feathers
if I could. I'm middle-aged and plump.
Back on dry land I shouldn't think these things:
big paws which idly turn to bat the air,
my face by his ribs and the purr which ripples
through the boards of the afterdeck,
the roar – even at a distance – ringing in my bones,
the rough tongue, the claws, the little bites,
the crude taste of his mane. If you touched my lips
with salt water I would tell you such words,
words to crack the sky and launch the ark again.

Life

My life as a bat
is for hearing
the world.

If I pitch it right
I can hear
just where you are.

If I pitch it right
I can hear inside your body:
the state of your health,

and more, I can hear
into your mind.
Bat death is not listening.

My life as a frog
is for touching
other things.

I'm very moist
so I don't get stuck
in the water.

I'm very moist
so I can cling
onto your back

for three days
and nights.
Frog death is separation.

My life as an iguana
is for tasting
everything

My tongue is very fast
because the flavour
of the air is so subtle.

It's long enough
to surprise
the smallest piece of you

from extremely
far away.
Iguana death is a closed mouth.

Rattlesnake

My rattlesnake has warm skin.
He sleeps by my feet and rustles
through my dreams, his diamond
back glistening all night.

Better than a fat alarm clock
is his subtle rattle at seven,
his cool glide towards breakfast,
his little fangs clinking the tea cup.

Cabbage Dreams

After dark, cabbages are proud and brilliant,
supercool. We stalk the garden
under the moon discussing politics with flowers.
We inspect your houses in the early hours
criticising the curtains, wondering about
the furniture, amazed at your reading habits.
Your clothes baffle us though we know
about layers and the colour of leaves.
We stare at your flabby fingers while
you sleep, speculate about your hairstyles.
Daytimes we fall back into ourselves,
sit around in vegetable racks, clutch
stubby leaves round our green shoulders
and hope you remember our sweet hearts.

Pig

You think of me
as clean and tasty,
don't want to know
about the mud, the tail,
the terrible trotters

don't want to know
about the neat little hats
in my wardrobe, the orchid
collection and the lengths and lengths
of breaststroke, the days and nights
in the Railtrack buffet
and the mad rapture for molluscs.

Hedgehog

The road is slick
in the rain
and good slugs
can be nuzzled
out of shadows
under hedgerows.

I understand.

It's plain
you can't hurry across
even when those other lights
come at you
preceding
the hurtling mountain.

Rhinoceros

What else to do
with the rhinoceros inside me
but feed him up with good hay,

cream his rough hide
with almond oil
until it gleams,

polish the two horns
on his face
with beeswax,

rinse his scaly feet
in rosewater;
once prepared

let him find the deepest pit
of mud inside my heart
and let him roll, roll, roll.

Elephant Woman

Nothing left except to grow
into my elephant skin,
expand into the great folds,

unfurl my ears across the kitchen,
remove myself into the bathroom
for nine days to celebrate my nose

and with my generous feet
tread gingerly round the house.

The Mad Cow in Space

Down there is little England, London, a dose
of crazy vision showing me a row
of heads on spikes outside the Tower. Still rotten,
still beautiful but ruined for me, now
I've seen stars with no atmosphere in the way.
Millions are on the Underground, going to work.
I can see them too, teeming just under
the Earth's crust. I'm weightless. Couldn't
fall over if you pushed me for a year.
The silence is an uproar and I write
with a special pen in which the ink can flow
without gravity to drag it to the page.
I'm trying to escape the pull myself:
don't want to look back at the Earth or send
more messages down to base about the way
it looks from here. Believe me, every smash,
every shot, every crack and blast is visible
and going right to plan but I can't stand
the Earth's screams as the blood touches her prissy skirt.

The Mad Cow is a *Vogue* Model

Giovanni, trained in Paris, has now spent
twenty-three minutes making me up.
Never before have I shown my whole body,
the full length of my combed-out tail, the visible
panty line, the unfurled rump to you,
my public. The photographer has planted me
in deep white space with perspective muddled on purpose.
I can't stand up straight. He doesn't understand
that I fall over sometimes and, anyway,
leaning is natural. But this is *Vogue*
where the upright and obedient send out
for anything they like. The Statue of Liberty
might do better. She is over three-
hundred feet high from torch to foundation.
Made of copper sheets beaten out by hand,
her first name was Liberty Enlightening the World.
She stands up straight without trying, but then
four gigantic steel supports run through her body.
And what will be at stake in this photo?
It's not an explicit language, but look
how I am snarling at the photographer.
I am snarling at his lens and through it a world
which wants my teeth, my eyes, my taste – and not
these words, these little deaths, these individual
devils, these visions of the whole damned lot.

Cheetah Run

I whisper, 'I'm coming baby,' to the distant hare
though my head's turned the full 180° away.
'Wait for me, no, run,' I shout because
I don't know which is more exciting, until
I'm accelerating into the full blast
of hare scent, grinning helplessly in the flood of it,
feeling my claws extend. My muscles
tug at me, and the tufts and tangles of longer
hair where my limbs join the torso.
Going after it like this, maybe I'd look more polite
if I kept my eyes on my own twitchy paws
or anywhere but where they want to go
towards the fine-tuned smell, the crunch of bone,
the blood at last as I turn to see his pain.

Drafts

The wind must be blowing
at Gale Force Ten. I have to lean
just to stay upright.
Either this gust

can shout louder than me
or it's made my own words fall
up into the air.
Perhaps I'll follow.

Northern Lights

We watched the islands from the waterfront
as though they held a clue to what was next.
The wind built up in gusts to match our hearts
and blew the café chairs into the water.

Police in boats fished out the furniture
with poles, making us laugh until the chuckles
rolled through us like the whale's back
rolls through water, like the islands

stretch through the north seas. I have stolen
some of the light which drenches you this midnight
to wish you all the islands in the world
and every one a different kind of peace.

Mandrake Pie

At home and abroad, we English brag about pie.
Our sailors bring home not just those heart-shaped boxes
crusted with little shells, but pie-cutters carved in doldrum days.

Implements of bone, one, two, or fabulously three-wheeled,
but always true, they allow fancy lattice-cutting back home
where no girl is marriageable until her pastry is so translucent

a sailor can read his tabloid right through it. Mandrake,
smelly, dangerous root of wonderful virtues, makes
the queen of pies, gives women babies and holds the wisdom

of the screaming dead. Pull your mandrake at dawn, double root
said to have grown from seeds of murderers put to death.
Ignore the shrieks as you tug and the scent that turns you on.

Bake it in the hottest oven you can get to make the air expand,
the pastry rise, as light as babies' breath. Ease the dough
into the tin, fill to the brim with the rough-chopped root,

and sprinkle with milk and water. Cover with pastry; seal
with a fork and then, and only then, may you lightly prick the
surface of your pie all over to let the screams escape.

A Visit from Janey

Janey wants to wreck my bathroom she's
so out of it. She's staggering towards
the unexpected wall of glass, waving
her bottle of booze, she's raiding the cabinet
for pills and screaming at the limescale stains
in the bath. The echo suits her voice so she smiles
and sits with a bump on the wooden toilet seat,
then grins up at the overhead cistern,
as she slips her beaded dress over her head.
So here's her stocky body, her small girl shape
slumped and naked on my toilet.
And now she's resonating my white tiles,
vibrating my roomy old bath: 'O Lord,'
she croons to the limescale, 'O Lord,' to the tap
which drips, 'O Lord,' to the overhead cistern,
cold porcelain, on which is gathering
the magic condensation of her breath.

Brünhilde

Brünhilde is not a young
woman. She is as old as
God and much heavier. I
am vanquished by her purple
quilted slippers, the way a
whiff of boiled kidney slips from
both the insoles when she walks.
I want to drink out of them,
a good strong rioja with
its own tang set off by hers.
She doesn't insert curlers
but I intend to make her.
They must all be dusty pink:
many of the little prongs
must be worn away or snipped
off leaving small prickly nubs
that catch at my skin when I
nibble her ear. O but her
perfume must be old piss and
Pledge, and I will be her dog,
wear her stiff nylon housecoat;
Brünhilde with her penchant
for Silk Cut, the French poems of
Rilke, her instinct for the
most vivid ways to ripen,
the most vivid ways to rot.

Watching Medusa

Struck dumb when I saw
her scalp begin to stir,

saw the little eyes slide
like drops through her hair,

saw them look back at me
kindly and fluid

as a bunch of lovers.
I cannot speak or move

in case I do wrong to her and
close the sweet hissing mouths.

To Rotterdam for the Rosie B. Babes

Even the children are dancing and in the foyer
of the nightclub the ornamental fish are restless.
I've been ten hours getting to Rotterdam
but Rose on tenor sax gives it some throat
as specialist dancers turn out in black and white
for some low-slung, loose-kneed jiving. We drink Grolsch
for free because my sweetie knows the barman.
Rose says, 'I've been singing that song for twenty years
and still don't know what it means.' Well I can tell her.
It means lights on in Rotterdam and shine
on the grubby buildings, the ferocious port.
It means Rose, two saxes, trumpet, and trombone,
piano, traps and bass, all peeling back
layers of occupation, layers of blitz;
Rose folding sea walls and reclaimed land,
rolling up canals. It means the North Sea
swallowing the whole damned lot as Rosie
sings again *My Funny Valentine*.

Framed

She enters the movie from nowhere as all stars do,
to lean against the rail, dab the fuchsia towel
with the palm of her little hand to dry the sweat.
Behind her, the salmon-pink double garage door
starts to open outwards and we hear
the rumble of a glossy car. She turns,
and her cheekbone cuts an arc against the sky.
Her eyes pan up and our shot follows them,
up, up the planted hill, past the blue roofs
the needle firs and the unreal palms, past the cacti
and the pink blossoms, past the skyline sun
and the few words of script behind a cloud,
to the corner of bare canvas right above her
which proves the sky is always the wrong way round.

Parsnip Cardiology

Every Christmas, he buys parsnips.
Parsnips for roasting, loads of them, suddenly;
for boiling to mash with the mash; for flinging

into the turkey stock; for glowing creamy pale in the dark;
for somehow being always cold to his touch when raw;
for peeling noisily and crunching hard against the knife;

for staining once in the air; for being a member of the
carrot family, but sweeter; for being mud-specked and
    wrinkled
and sprouting hair roots, yet altogether sound, with a core
    straight

through. But he may not be like that, after all, tomorrow
when they listen to his blood, listen for the flaw
in the valve that might stop his heart too soon.

Lovebirds

So she moved into the hospital the last nine days
to tend him with little strokes and murmurs
as he sank into the sheets. Nurse
set out a low bed for her, night-times, next to his.
He nuzzled up to her as she brushed
away the multiplying cells with a sigh,
was glad as she ignored the many
effluents and the tang of death. The second
last morning of his life he opened
his eyes, saying, 'I can't wake up'
but wouldn't close them for his nap
until he was sure she was there.
Later he moved quietly to deeper sleep,
as Doctor said he would, still listening
to her twittering on and on until the last.

When I Died

I'm coming back on All Saints' Day
for your olives, old peanuts and dodgy sherry,
dirty dancing. I'll cross-dress at last
pirouette and flash, act pissed.
You'll have to look for me hard:
search for my bones in the crowd.
Or lay a pint and a pie on my grave to tempt me out
and a trail of marigolds back to the flat,
where you'll leave the door ajar
and the cushions plumped in my old armchair.

Professional Mourner

First I'll shave my head and take the phone off the hook.
I'll be close to madness so be sure not to speak
to me in case I infect you with crazy talk.
Fireworks, pipers and the mixing desk, all extra,
but loud, really loud, lamentation is basic.
Once excessive crying turned me blind for two whole days.
If you prefer I can be more silent, even,
than the dear departed: watch me speak in the sign-
language of the dead, catching my tears in muslin
nets before they crash to the floor. The job's diverse:
for you I'll kill a mouse, flay it and tap dance
with its little pelt around the open grave.
Please don't mind when I fling shit about, hurl insults,
copulate with granddad, molest your sister,
glue my crotch to your leg and drink the coffin dry.
'I am drunk! I am an animal!' I'll cry
as I steal the body, try to ransom it, take off
my skin and drape it over the coffin. Last seen,
riff-backing up the aisle in just my bones.

Spaghetti Junction

after Hans Magnus Enzensberger

Ranting, belted up and bitter, if it's not the leather heated
seats, it's the stonking space frame chassis, the abuse overtaking
and all that knowing about insurance, scarce spare parts,
then the traffic jam, the blue light, the stretcher.

From below you're watching instruments wink, you're slanting
under the alternative light of the anaesthetic.
The sister's uniform is white; she's well into her TV.
   Headphones.
Dramas you can't hear flicker over her dark face.

A gear crunches in the brain. Rear-view mirror,
signal, manoeuvre but don't look now. Central locking.
Even screaming hurts. Little bubbles rise,
glass marbles, in the intravenous drip.

The traffic clears; you're really motoring. The double
wishbone independent suspension's a tad spongy but then
spring rates, bushing stiffnesses and geometries equal
roadholding fantastic. Everything's stereo, the drumroll,

stereo, heartbeat, the hiss of oxyacetylene
cutting the ditched wreck open in blue, the pat, pat
of mud falling later, falling from the spade splat on
that place between cracked eyes where your spectacles once sat.

Motherland

after Tsvetaèva

Language is impossible
in a country like this. Even
the dictionary laughs when I look up
'England', 'Motherland', 'Home'.

It insists on falling open instead
three times out of the nine I try it
at the word Distance. *Degree
of remoteness, interval of space.*

Distance: the word is ingrained like pain.
So much for England and so much
for my future to walk into the horizon
carrying distance in a broken suitcase.

The dictionary is the only one
who talks to me now. Says, laughing,
'Come back HOME!' but takes me
further and further away into the cold stars.

I am blue, bluer than water
I am nothing, while all I do
is waste syllables this way.

England. It hurts my lips to shape
the word. This country makes me say
too many things I can't say. Home
of me, myself, my motherland.

A Letter to Dennis

in memoriam Dennis Potter

Deep in the strangest pits in England, deep
in the strangest forest, my grandfathers
and yours coughed out their silicotic lungs.
Silicosis. England. Land of phlegm
and stereophonic gobbing, whose last pearls
of sputum on the lips, whose boils and tropes
and hallucinations are making me sick.

The point is how to find a use for fury,
as you have taught, old father,
my old butt, wherever you are.
Still rude, I hope, still raucous and rejoicing
in the most painful erection in heaven
which rises through its carapace of sores
and cracking skin to sing in English.

You are as live to me as the tongue
in my mouth, as the complicated shame
of Englishness. Would you call me lass?
Would you heave up any stars for my crown?